Endorsements for the Cl

"Christians are pressed by very real questions. How does Scripture structure a church, order worship, organize ministry, or define biblical leadership? Those are just examples of the questions that are answered clearly, carefully, and winsomely in this new series from 9Marks. I am so thankful for this ministry and for its incredibly healthy and hopeful influence in so many faithful churches. I eagerly commend this series."

R. Albert Mohler Jr., President, The Southern Baptist Theological Seminary

"Sincere questions deserve thoughtful answers. If you're not sure where to start in answering these questions, let this series serve as a diving board into the pool. These minibooks are winsomely to-the-point and great to read together with one friend or one hundred friends."

Gloria Furman, author, *Missional Motherhood* and *The Pastor's Wife*

"As a pastor, I get asked lots of questions. I'm approached by unbelievers seeking to understand the gospel, new believers unsure about next steps, and maturing believers wanting help answering questions from their Christian family, friends, neighbors, or coworkers. It's in these moments that I wish I had a book to give them that was brief, answered their questions, and pointed them in the right direction for further study. Church Questions is a series that provides just that. Each booklet tackles one question in a biblical, brief, and practical manner. The series may be called Church Questions, but it could be called 'Church Answers.' I intend to pick these up by the dozens and give them away regularly. You should too."

Juan R. Sanchez, Senior Pastor, High Pointe Baptist Church, Austin, Texas

"Where can we Christians find reliable answers to our common questions about life together at church—without having to plow through long, expensive books? The Church Questions booklets meet our need with answers that are biblical, thoughtful, and practical. For pastors, this series will prove a trustworthy resource for guiding church members toward deeper wisdom and stronger unity."

Ray Ortlund, President, Renewal Ministries

How Can I
Be Sure I'm
Saved?

Church Questions

How Can I
Be Sure I'm
Saved?

Jeremy Pierre

WHEATON, ILLINOIS

How Can I Be Sure I'm Saved?

Copyright © 2022 by 9Marks

Published by Crossway
        1300 Crescent Street
        Wheaton, Illinois 60187

Cover image and design: Jordan Singer

First printing 2022

Printed in the United States of America

Trade paperback ISBN: 978-1-4335-7867-0
ePub ISBN: 978-1-4335-7870-0
PDF ISBN: 978-1-4335-7868-7
Mobipocket ISBN: 978-1-4335-7869-4

Library of Congress Cataloging-in-Publication Data

Names: Pierre, Jeremy, 1979- author.
Title: How can I be sure I'm saved? / Jeremy Pierre.
Description: Wheaton, Illinois : Crossway, [2022] | Series: Church questions | Includes bibliographical references and index.
Identifiers: LCCN 2021048679 (print) | LCCN 2021048680 (ebook) | ISBN 9781433578670 (trade paperback) | ISBN 9781433578687 (pdf) | ISBN 9781433578694 (mobipocket) | ISBN 9781433578700 (epub)
Subjects: LCSH: Assurance (Theology) | Salvation—Christianity.
Classification: LCC BT785 .P54 2022 (print) | LCC BT785 (ebook) | DDC 234—dc23/eng/20211118
LC record available at https://lccn.loc.gov/2021048679
LC ebook record available at https://lccn.loc.gov/2021048680

Crossway is a publishing ministry of Good News Publishers.

BP		31	30	29	28	27	26	25	24	23	22
15	14	13	12	11	10	9	8	7	6	5	4	3	2	1

Blessed be the God and Father of our Lord Jesus Christ, who has blessed us in Christ with every spiritual blessing in the heavenly places, even as he chose us in him before the foundation of the world, that we should be holy and blameless before him. In love he predestined us for adoption to himself as sons through Jesus Christ, according to the purpose of his will, to the praise of his glorious grace, with which he has blessed us in the Beloved.

Ephesians 1:3–6

If the Christian life were charted on a map, the starting point could be labeled "God loves you." The blue line tracing the path from that point would turn, curve, and eventually arch its way back to that very same point. The Christian journey is a long, difficult path back to the place you started—the place you realized that, despite your sin, *God loves you.*

Why a path back to the same place? That's in part what this little book is about. It's a journey every Christian takes. We each take it individually, but that doesn't mean we take it alone. It sometimes *feels* lonely, especially if you're in the middle of a struggle to know if you're really saved. You may have picked up this book because you just aren't sure where you stand with the Lord. Maybe you look around at other Christians and wonder why they seem so assured and why you don't share in that assurance. You may wonder if you're some different species of Christian or not a Christian at all. If you were really God's child, wouldn't he want you to be assured of his love too?

That last question is the key one. Like all people created in the image of God, you were made to be loved by God and to love him in return. This is your chief purpose. *God loves me* ought to be at the center of the human soul. Everything works right when this love is in place, and everything goes wrong when it's hindered. So when you aren't assured of his love—and when you find your own heart unable to love him in return—your very identity starts coming apart.

Maybe these words seem too dramatic. If so, consider yourself blessed. The Lord has kindly chosen to make the degree of your struggle with assurance less than others' struggles. But if these words don't feel dramatic, if you know the distress of feeling unloved by God, then you need to know you're not alone. The path may feel lonely to you, but Christians throughout history have labored through these valleys, where God seems unwilling to assure them personally of his love. And so they cry out, *why?*

No individual can know for sure why he lacks assurance of God's love. But in the countless conversations I've had with Christians in these gloomy valleys, I find they generally presume one of two causes: either great sin or great suffering.

Maybe a person is convinced he's too sinful to be loved by a holy God. He knows the shame of his secret sins. He's tortured by the perverted thoughts that seem to intrude constantly on his mind. He might be cynical and harsh toward others, in his heart more than with his mouth. Even his thoughts about God himself are off— sometimes lifeless and dull, sometimes outright blasphemous. He knows that if people saw what *really* went on inside him, they would agree that a holy God should reject him. And so he closes in on himself, fearful of anyone finding out his dark struggle.

Or maybe a person is so overwhelmed with suffering she wonders how she could be loved by the God who claims to be compassionate. Fresh troubles keep coming into her life, so she cries out to the Lord for help. But God seems deaf to her. She knows from Scripture that God hears his children when they cry to him, so the conclusion is inevitable. When she drops hints to other Christians about her pain, they offer little more than a vague promise to pray. Loneliness and depression leave her without strength. She knows God has plenty of strength to spare but apparently not for her.

Maybe you can relate to one or both of these reasons. Maybe your sin and your suffering seem near, and God's love seems far. Whatever the cause of these valleys for an individual believer, the struggle with assurance is real, and it is an expression of a bigger issue.

Here's the bigger issue and the main point of this little book: Your struggle with assurance is a struggle to see yourself rightly. More specifically, it's the struggle to exchange your perspective of yourself with God's perspective of you. It involves settling your mind not on *certainty* but on *trust*. Trust is relational, meaning that you rely on God to be the one who loves you first and foremost, with your love only an imperfect response. God's love is expressed to believers by all three persons of the Trinity—the Father, Son, and Holy Spirit. Christians receive this love through the word, prayer, and fellowship with the church. In fact, you learn to see yourself in light of this love not on your own but among God's people.

I'll break down this main point in three sections: (1) *learning to see yourself as God does*, (2) *the unprovoked love of the Triune God*, and (3) *trusting that God loves you*.

Learning to See Yourself as God Does

Main Point, Part 1: *Your struggle with assurance is a struggle to see yourself rightly—specifically, to exchange your perspective of yourself with God's perspective of you. It involves settling your mind not on certainty but on trust.*

A struggle with assurance is about self-perception. Behind the question "How can I know that I am saved?" is the broader question "How do I know anything about myself?"

You could call this an identity question. Personal identity can be described in two parts: perception and reality. *Perception* is who you think you are. *Reality* is who you actually are. Learning to see the distinction between the two is part of maturing as a person and as a Christian. It means acknowledging that *how you see yourself* may or may not line up with *who you are*. Actually, a better way to say that might be: *how you see yourself* in part lines up with *who you are* and in part does not. How do you know the difference?

Ultimately, you can only know the difference by learning to listen to the God who made you. He alone knows you as you actually are. Assurance comes from learning to submit your subjective perspective of self to God's objective understanding of you.

This guidance takes place over a lifetime of learning to listen to what God says about you.

This is how the gospel addresses both the reality of *who you are* and your perception, *how you see yourself*. God uses both Scripture and fellowship with other believers to align our perceptions with reality. In Scripture, we have God's own words, which display his heart toward sinners and sufferers of every stripe. You're no exception. In fellowship, we see other believers model the right kind of self-perception: humble confidence that God really is as generous to undeserving people as he claims to be. They have to figure themselves out no less than you do. You're no exception there either.

But here's what may be the hardest part of the assurance question—and really any identity question. The only reliable answer will come not as *certainty* but as *trust*.

The desire for certainty is the longing to know beyond the possibility of doubt. It's the desire for knowledge so absolute you possess it on your own. It can never be questioned or reconsidered. In other words, the desire for certainty is the yearning to know something objectively *as it is*. But the problem with this desire is that you are wanting to know something in a way only God can know (Deut. 29:29; Ps. 139:6).

As a creature, your knowledge of things is limited. But God the Creator has no limits on his knowledge. You know some things imperfectly yet truly. But God knows everything perfectly and fully. Your ability to know is *dependent*, while God's is *independent*. What that means is only God can attain the kind of *certainty* that someone who struggles with assurance might be obsessing over. If you think you can only settle your mind if you know you are saved beyond the shadow of a doubt, then your mind will never be settled.

This is actually good news. God did not design you with such an unattainable standard of knowledge. What is attainable to people, however, is *knowledgeable trust*. It's a knowledge that is dependent on what God says about his heart toward sinners and sufferers, including you. Your local church is full of such people who have to depend on God in the same way.

Knowledgeable trust is the correct standard of knowing. The apostle John describes this trust tenderly in his letter to uncertain Christians. The letter is filled with the phrase "By this we know," referring to one's personal standing with God (1 John 2:3, 5; 3:16, 24; 4:2, 6, 16; 5:2). But perhaps the two most prominent expressions— like two lookout points on a mountain that give you a sweeping overview—are found in 1 John 3 and 1 John 5. Consider the first lookout point:

> By this we shall know that we are of the truth and reassure our heart before him; for whenever our heart condemns us, God is greater than our heart, and he knows everything. Beloved, if our heart does not condemn us, we have confidence before God. (1 John 3:19–21)

Here John acknowledges that Christians— who *objectively* belong to God—can *subjectively* experience seasons when their view of self doesn't line up with the reality of who they are. He gives two contrasting phrases: "whenever our heart condemns us" and "if our heart does not condemn us." Both are possible for a genuine believer. Now, what is the solution to those times when our perception of self condemns us—that is, when we see ourselves as outside salvation? John makes a simple theological contrast between God's knowledge and ours: "God is greater than our heart, and he knows everything."

This means God knows, better than you do, who you are—*everything* about you. The ugliest thoughts, the sickest fantasies, the cynicism, the hate, the emotional chaos, the corrupted motivations. He knows better than your own heart knows how undeserving of salvation you are. Yet, there he is, reminding you how Jesus defends sinners like you (1 John 2:1–2), how fear melts away as you realize that God's love came before yours ever could (4:18–19), and how confident you can be of God's generous heart when you approach him (5:13–15). God knows better than you how undeserving you are. This is true of every sinner equally. Yet he insists on proclaiming his love to anyone who will listen. Including you. This is how John compels you to *knowledgeable trust* in the one who knows all things as they are.

The second lookout reiterates the same point. These words close John's letter:

> And we know that the Son of God has come and has given us understanding, so that we may know him who is true; and we are in him who is true, in his Son Jesus Christ. He is the true God and eternal life. (1 John 5:20)

Where does your understanding come from? The Son of God himself has come and *has given us understanding*. Your understanding of yourself is not independent certainty, not settled fact that you possess in yourself. No, your knowledge, even of yourself, is dependent on the Son of God coming to earth to give access to knowledge you don't have on your own. John drives this point home by reminding you of the contrast between you and Jesus: "He is the true God and eternal life." The true God is the only one in the universe whose knowledge doesn't depend on anyone else's. You can't say that about yourself. Your view of yourself depends on his view of you.

So, *how can I know . . . ?* It is a struggle to base your confidence not on an internal sense of sureness but on the claims of another. You cannot know with independent certainty. So stop trying to get it by obsessing about your salvation. Stop criticizing yourself for not being able to reach it. Stop panicking because you assume other Christians have it. Stop trying to know things in a way only God can. Instead, trust that when the Apostle John penned these words, God knew your eyes would eventually read an English translation of them. Be willing to bank everything you believe about *yourself* on what God says about *himself*—that his heart toward sinners and sufferers is as generous as he claims.

The Unprovoked Love of the Triune God

Main Point, Part 2: *Trust is relational, meaning that you rely on God to be the one who loves you first and foremost, with your love only an imperfect response. God's love is expressed to believers by all three persons of the Trinity—the Father, Son, and Holy Spirit.*

The previous section hopefully helped you understand the difference between the subjective and the objective aspects of salvation. You are called to trust *not* in your perception but in God's heart displayed in his actions on behalf of sinners.

In other words, salvation is a bigger reality than your experience of it. This section will help you understand this larger reality, so you can get outside your head and trust in something bigger.

And here's that bigger reality: God's love was not caused by you, and it cannot be uncaused by you. You cannot cause God to love you by your worthiness, and you cannot cause God to unlove you by your unworthiness. It is so ancient, so powerful, so permanent that no creature can provoke it. Love is part of his very nature as Triune God. In fact—and this should deeply impress you—all three persons of the Trinity are active in God's love for sinners—and more specifically, in their love for you. Consider this.

God is your Father, and he loved you before you had the chance to be unlovable.

J. I. Packer said, "Love among men is awakened by something in the beloved, but the love of God is free, spontaneous, unevoked, uncaused. God loves men because he has chosen to love them."[1] By *men* here, Packer means *individuals*. I point that out not merely to emphasize that God's love is not gender-specific (though what a wonderful truth that men and women equally belong in the beloved) but rather that the eternal love of God is placed on specific individuals. And nothing those individuals do provokes this love.

Scripture tells us that God made the choice to love each of his children before he even formed the world they'd eventually occupy (Eph. 1:4). Before he created the air their lungs would need, he determined to love them. Before that oxygen would fuel a single action, good or bad, his purpose to show individual grace was set (2 Tim. 1:9). God loved you before you had the chance to be unlovable. He beat you to the punch. He came first.

In fact, this is the key to overcoming the fear of being condemned by God: God is first. The generosity of his love comes *before* the offense of your sin. That is a *before* of both time and priority. God chooses to show his greatness in beating everyone to the punch. He loves sinners prior to any chance of them loving him in return. The apostle John wrote, "There is no fear in love, but perfect love casts out fear. For fear has to do with punishment, and whoever fears has not been perfected in love. We love because he first loved us" (1 John 4:18–19).

Your heavenly Father comes first. His love is self-caused, not you-caused. This is in large part why the first person of the Trinity refers to himself as Father. Fathers come before sons and daughters. Perhaps you need to humble yourself under the greatness of a Father who came first. He is free to do as he pleases, unconstrained even by your resistance.

Jesus is your righteousness, and he makes you right despite your many wrongs.

You may be painfully aware of what's wrong with you, burdened by those old sinful habits that draw you back so powerfully. You look inside yourself and see transgression, and it burns. The thought of your heart being clean and pure is a lovely but impossible sentiment. Righteousness does not characterize your private life and often not your public one. If this is your honest assessment, your gloomy confession, you may be closer than you think to that bright and shining righteousness.

The apostle John says, "If we say we have no sin, we deceive ourselves, and the truth is not in us. If we confess our sins, he is faithful and just to forgive us our sins and to cleanse us from all unrighteousness" (1 John 1:8–9). To confess simply means to agree with God about our sin. It's as bad as he says it is, and it's no one's fault but ours.

But consider the outcome: the faithful and just God forgives and cleanses us of exactly that unrighteousness. How can this be? "But if anyone does sin, we have an advocate with the Father, Jesus Christ the righteous" (2:1). Jesus becomes righteousness *for you*. Get this: Jesus is the one who contributes the righteousness. You only contribute sin. But Christians contribute *confessed* sin—sin that's uncovered, exposed, agreed upon.

John Bunyan suffered frequent storms in his soul regarding assurance. He wrote about it often, describing various milestones on his journey of assurance. In his memoir, the aptly titled *Grace Abounding to the Chief of Sinners*, he described walking outside, passing through a field. In that moment, he felt heavy under the guilt of his sin. But a sentence flashed through his mind: *Thy righteousness is in heaven*. And he thought of Christ at God's right hand, proclaiming himself as Bunyan's righteousness. And then Bunyan realized that God could not say of him, "This Bunyan fellow lacks my righteousness." Why? Because it was right there in front of him. Here's how he ends his account:

> I also saw moreover, that it was not my good frame of heart that made my righteousness better, nor yet my bad frame that made my righteousness worse: for my righteousness was Jesus Christ himself, *the same yesterday, and today, and for ever* (Heb. 13:8).[2]

The love of Jesus is powerful because he is righteous—so righteous that he can *be* the righteousness of anyone who trusts in him. Including you.

The Holy Spirit is your Comforter, and he helps you hear Jesus when you can only hear yourself.

Sometimes one of the worst voices to listen to is your own, especially when the topic of conversation is *you*. Even Christians flip-flop between self-hate and self-justification. You can go from thinking you're all set to thinking you're done for, all in an afternoon. Whatever the message, listening to your own voice about yourself is a risky thing to do.

Thankfully, God gives us his Holy Spirit to help with this:

> For you did not receive the spirit of slavery to fall back into fear, but you have received the Spirit of adoption as sons, by whom we cry, "Abba! Father!" The Spirit himself bears witness with our spirit that we are children of God, and if children, then heirs—heirs of God and fellow heirs with Christ, provided we suffer with him

in order that we may also be glorified with
him. (Rom. 8:15–17)

Notice something. Paul anticipated fear as
part of the Christian experience. He knew a
Christian is in a conflict between two *spirits*—
or identities that direct how a person lives. The
spirit of slavery identifies you as enslaved, lead-
ing you to obey sin as your master. To counter
this false identity, the Spirit "bears witness with
our spirit." To *bear witness* is to testify, to speak
to the truth of something. He declares that you
were adopted out of the slave family you came
from by a free family—and not merely a free
family but a royal family. You are no longer a
slave but a child of God.

Being a child of God doesn't mean that you
live in a posh palace—at least not yet. As a royal
child, you will one day inherit freedom beyond
your wildest imagining. But for now, you suffer.
And the *suffering with Christ* Paul refers to here
is the suffering of resistance. You are resisting
the pull back into sin, back into your old slavery.
You see, straining for assurance isn't merely a

struggle for psychological peace. It's a struggle to believe what the Spirit testifies about both *you* and, more importantly, about *Christ*.

The Spirit's job is to remind you of Jesus's words about himself and his intention to save sinners just like you (John 14:25–31). Satan's accusations against you and your accusations against yourself will be really loud at times. But the Holy Spirit has a stronger voice. Trust what he says.

How do you strengthen that trust? I just reminded you of the Father's eternal determination to love sinners like you, Jesus's ability to make you righteous despite your profound unrighteousness, and the Spirit's determination to speak over the noise about Christ's love for you. But practically, how does this express itself in your life?

Trusting That *God Loves You*

Main Point, Part 3: *Christians receive this love through the word, prayer, and fellowship with the church. In fact, you learn to* *see yourself in light of this love not on your own but among God's people.*

You'll remember from the opening of this little book that the Christian life is a journey back to the point where you began. That point is labeled simply "God loves you." The journey is moving from understanding the love of God as a doctrine to receiving it personally for yourself. That deeper reception is called trust—an increasingly wholehearted surrender to God's love.

Surrendering to God is active not passive. Even though you are *passive* in causing God's love, you are *active* in responding to it. In other words, you are passive in your justification and regeneration and adoption but active in your response to those wonderful realities. This closing section is my attempt to convince you that the best way to strengthen personal trust in God's love for you is to seek out the places he speaks most clearly of this love: *in his word, in prayer, and in his people.*

I'll provide principles in this section to guide your active pursuit of assurance, but you must not think of these as a measured step-by-step process that leads to a measurable outcome. Sinclair Ferguson writes,

> Some discover assurance after long battles; others never know what it is to be without it; for some it comes through sorrows, for others through joy. It is as individual as it is sovereign, and necessarily so, because it leads us to say, "The Son of God, who *loved me* and gave himself *for me*."[3]

With this pastoral word in mind, let me offer some humble guidance for your active pursuit of assurance. My goal is not merely to tell you *to* read the word, pray, and seek fellowship but rather *how to* read the word, pray, and seek fellowship.

1. Read the Word as if God wants to assure you of salvation, not assure you of condemnation.

God speaks in order to save. Or, as John Webster puts it, "Revelation is reconciliation."[4]

The purpose of God speaking to people is to bring salvation to those who listen. To read

Scripture faithfully, you must read it in light of this primary purpose. Wherever you think you stand as an individual before God as you open the pages of Scripture, it's important that you recognize something: His purpose for speaking was established before you were born. You are not some special case. Humble yourself by recognizing that you are not the exception to God's purposes.

Ever since sin entered the world, the purpose of his words to humanity is to save anyone who listens. If he wanted to condemn people, he would not need to speak to them. He would simply carry out his righteous judgment. But Scripture is one long story of God speaking to humanity for the purpose of committing himself to act for their salvation. From the opening chapters of Scripture, God uses words for this central purpose: "God commits himself to a course of faithful action that leads up to the birth of Christ and the pouring out of the Spirit at Pentecost and continues through the present 'last days' right up until the future return of Christ."[5] You know what this shows? The matter of your personal salvation is much bigger than your opinion about yourself. It has to do with God's purposes in Christ to take the action necessary to save anyone who believes.

So you must read all of Scripture—even the frightening parts—in light of God's committed action. Even the most alarming warning passages, such as Hebrews 6:4–8 or 12:15–17, are intended to bring salvation, not condemnation. How do you know this? Because you only warn someone you want to save. If you hear God's voice in these passages, you will heed his warning and grab hold of Jesus Christ as the only way to face the fire of judgment and not be burned.

You may be wondering, "Well, how do I know that I've grabbed hold of Jesus in this way?" Perhaps you're ultra-aware of what I mentioned earlier in John's first letter—that a true Christian, as opposed to those who only claim to be Christians, is characterized by obedience to God's commands, love for other believers, and rejection of the world's idols. Perhaps you look at your life and aren't sure you see enough of these features.

Well, let's face this straight on. Here's what John says:

> By this we know that we love the children of God, when we love God and obey his commandments. For this is the love of God, that we keep his commandments. And his commandments are not burdensome. For everyone who has been born of God overcomes the world. And this is the victory that overcomes the world—our faith. Who is it that overcomes the world except the one who believes that Jesus is the Son of God? (1 John 5:2–5)

What saves you? Your obedience to God, your love for believers, or your rejection of the world? Answer: none of those things. Rather, you are saved by Jesus, the Son of God, who is the fulfillment of God's commitment to act on behalf of sinners. It's why God speaks. Your only response is to trust what he says.

But you may still be haunted by the stubborn fear that God put Scripture in your hands to assure you of condemnation. But consider:

when God actually condemns sinners, he simply hands them over to their sin so they are unable to see it for themselves (Rom. 1:24, 26, 28). Their deafness to him is a sign of their condemnation. Insofar as you are alarmed by your sin and what it indicates about your standing before the Lord, you can still hear. You have not been handed over. If you think God is somehow torturing you by making sure you know your condemnation is guaranteed before it happens, you are not reading Scripture according to God's purpose to provoke sinners to run to him for salvation.

If God's word scares you about your sin, you need to understand this as *conviction* not *condemnation*. Trust that God is both willing and able to save you, just as he says in his word. Submit your perspective to his. Not sure how to do this? Well, along with listening to his word, you must speak to him in prayer.

2. Pray as if God knows better than you do about your salvation.

In prayer, we break free of small thoughts and open ourselves to bigger ones. Prayer is one of the main ways we give our fears to the Lord by expressing them to him, instead of allowing them to take over our minds. Think of it this way: We speak to ourselves about ourselves a lot. But the way to change self-talk is not merely with more self-talk. It's to speak to the Lord about ourselves. This is how we submit our perspective to his.

To do this well, you need to be specific about the thoughts you entertain about yourself, submitting them to God with specific truth you know from his word. Here are some examples of different prayer strategies that specifically identify, express, and ask the Lord for help in the specifics.

- I've asked God for assurance, but he does not give it. I can't be sure I'm saved.

  - **Identify:** What I want right now is certainty. But I should be wanting faith.
  - **Express:** Lord, only you can have the kind of certainty I'm wishing for myself, because only you know all

things as they are (Rom. 11:33–36).
I can't even know myself fully, and
so I need you to help me see myself
rightly.

- **Ask:** Lord, I do not ask for certainty
  but for faith to believe that you are
  as generous to me as you are to other
  sinners. You tell me that you are rich
  in mercy and full of a love so deep
  no one could deserve it. This is who
  you are, and I can trust you even
  about myself (Eph. 2:4–10).

- I am scared of God. I've upset him.

  - **Identify:** My fear is making me
    move away from God, not toward
    him. Satan is the author of this kind
    of fear, not God.

  - **Express:** Lord, my fear of you is
    making me run from you, not to
    you. You tell me that your love casts
    out the wrong kind of fear (1 John
    4:16–19) and replaces it with the
    right kind (1 Pet. 1:17–21).

- **Ask:** Lord, help me to fear you like
  I should, not be scared of you like I
  shouldn't. When I feel your anger,
  help me run *to* you instead of *away*
  from you. Your love means you will
  always receive me, no matter my
  wrongs (Luke 15:11–32).

- My sin is so shameful I can't possibly be saved.

  - **Identify:** My conscience is con-
    stantly accusing me. But the pur-
    pose of my conscience is to provoke
    me to confess sin as part of being
    forgiven. Anything short of this
    purpose is from Satan, the accuser.
  - **Express:** Lord, you know both the
    guilt of my sins and the shame of
    my sinfulness. Help me acknowl-
    edge it the right way, before you and
    your people. You tell me that when
    I uncover my sin, you cover it with
    something far better, the righteous-
    ness of your Son (Ps. 32:5–7; 1 John
    1:8–2:2).

- **Ask:** Shelter me from the accuser. Help me to face the earthly consequences of my sin with joyful resolve (Ps. 38; 2 Cor. 7:10–11) because the eternal consequences have been gloriously removed. There is no condemnation left for me, since Jesus took it from me (Rom. 8:1–4).

- I am not good enough to be loved by God. I'm a worthless disappointment.

  - **Identify:** I am claiming things about myself that God does not claim about me. I am assuming God's opinion of me matches my own opinion or that of others.
  - **Express:** Lord, I am very critical of myself and aware of other people's criticism of me. I can't escape a sense of being a disappointment. But you don't share these earthly standards of beauty or success. I am no *more* and no *less* worthy than

other sinners to receive salvation
(1 Cor. 1:27–29; Phil. 4:7).

- **Ask:** Lord, help me to humble myself before you by acknowledging
that you made me a fragile jar of
clay not to dispose of me but to fill
me with a power that is clearly not
from me (2 Cor. 4:7–10). You want
me never to be confident in myself
but only in your love for me (2 Cor.
12:7–10; Gal. 2:20).

*3. Seek fellowship as if God displays in
other Christians the kind of humble
assurance you can have too.*

Assurance of salvation is contagious.

That sentence might surprise you, since you
may feel the opposite when you go to church
and see everyone else singing their hearts out
to the Lord, testifying to his grace in their lives,
receiving the word with an eagerness that seems
absent from your experience. Maybe being
around believers makes you *less* assured that
you are saved.

If that's your experience, may I unearth a hidden problem that may be lurking in your perspective? You may be assuming that other Christians find assurance because they *don't* struggle as you do. But let me flip the script. What if they are finding assurance because they *do* struggle as you do? What if the confidence they express is not automatic to them but rather is forged by the very shame and doubt you're assuming is yours alone?

Do you see now how assurance of salvation can be contagious? You may have a wealth of Christians surrounding you who have wrestled with God through dark nights of insecurity and fear, only to emerge somehow blessed by him with assurance. The right kind of confidence in the love of God is contagious.

Here's why the church is so essential to your personal assurance of salvation: You live in a world of competing voices. These voices tell you what you ought to think about yourself, about other people, and most importantly about God himself. You *cannot not* listen to the voices that surround you (double negative intended). So here's the question: What voices do you surround yourself with?

If you've shied away from Christians because you think they have some quality you don't that makes them totally and perfectly assured, then you've gravitated somewhere else. Perhaps you've tried to distract yourself from the pain with other concerns like work or school, or amusements like sports or gaming, or other relationships with folks who don't seem bothered with the eternal questions that plague you. All of these pursuits involve different communities that tell you how to see yourself; they tell you how to answer—or ignore—the questions that haunt you. But these communities may only be helping you distract yourself from the real issue of where you stand before the Almighty God.

The only community able to support you on this most pressing question is the church. The church is the household of the living God, the place where the truth of Jesus is celebrated (1 Tim. 3:15–16). It's where the faith of one believer reinforces the faith of another (Rom. 1:12, 16–17). It's where Christians speak the truth about themselves and about their Savior to one another and thus grow—that is, make real progress—in their confidence in the love of God (Eph. 4:11–16).

Even more, we need to remember that Jesus authorized the local church to mark out the people of God. In Matthew 16, Jesus said the church holds the "keys of the kingdom of heaven." It's a complicated metaphor, but ultimately what Jesus means is that his local churches represent heaven and declare on heaven's behalf who belongs to that kingdom. How do churches do this? Through membership. When you're baptized into the name of the Father, Son, and Spirit, the church is essentially saying "We're confident this person belongs to Jesus." Not only that, everytime the church celebrates the Lord's Supper and invites your participation, they're saying "We're *still* confident this person belongs to Jesus." Of course, a person could have false assurance based *merely* on church membership or the Lord's Supper. But don't let that steal from the power behind these formal ways of being included in the church. Every time you take the

Lord's Supper with your church family, remember this: dozens, hundreds, or even thousands of other believers are expressing their confidence in your standing before the Lord, even when you lack that confidence yourself.

The church formally contributes to our assurance of salvation, but it helps us informally, too, through the relationships we forge in the community of God's people. Remember, personal assurance grows as a person trusts more fully in God's love, which results in her imitating that love in her life. Love for others, love for God's commands, and love for God himself are the responses to his love that build assurance in the experience of a believer. These expressions aren't in addition to faith but the expression of faith. And your church community is where these expressions take place.

If you've kept your struggle with assurance to yourself, here's my strongest advice: Don't. Don't shy away from the people of God. They're one of your greatest protections. Go talk to a pastor or a mature believer about what you've considered in this little book. You may find that even if they don't struggle with exactly the same issues you do, they have indeed struggled. And you will find that their confidence in the love of God is not *despite* this struggle but *because* of it.

A Parting Word from a Fellow Struggler

Much of what you've read here was forged in a season of my own life when it seemed to me that God was dangling me over the flames of judgment. By all outward appearances, I was doing great at the time—a deacon at my church, studying in seminary to become a pastor, faithful to my wife, and steady in my personal devotions.

But inside I was destitute of any sense that God loved me. Even as I look back on that season now, I don't fully know why it occurred. I wasn't captured by some secret sin. I wasn't flirting with any godless ideologies. I wasn't coming to terms with past losses. For whatever reason, I'd become ultra-aware of how profoundly self-centered I was, how even my pursuit of ministry was self-serving, how my love for everyone in my life depended on what they did for me. And at the center of it all was the blunt reality that I did not love God with all my heart—in fact, I loved him with barely a fraction of it.

For about three months I was convinced I did not love God at all and that he rightfully did not love me. God felt cold to my prayers, Scripture felt hot in its judgment, and church people seemed unable to understand. I was alone.

I wouldn't repeat that experience for all the fame and fortune in the world. I mean that literally. It was hell compressed into twelve weeks. But that agony produced something in me. I remember lying on the floor of my bedroom, crying out again and again to the God who didn't love me. In those prayers, I rehearsed to God the truths I'd heard preached and sung and prayed at my church—truths that seemed to be for everyone in those pews but me. Then, in exhaustion, I found myself resigning to my fate, saying, "God, if you are going to send me to hell, you're going to have to do it with me clinging to Jesus's feet."

And for the first time in a long time, I felt warmth flicker in my heart. In the face of the

judgment I believed was before me, I had de-
clared, however pitifully, that Jesus was my only
confidence that God should love me. And in a
moment, it dawned on me that the love I hadn't
been able to perceive might have been there all
along.

My struggle didn't completely evaporate
that evening, but from that point I began to see
more clearly that God was using this agony to
convince me more deeply that my salvation was
caused by nothing other than his unprovoked,
undeserved, and unending love. I needed him
to love me first and to love me last. Today, I'm
even more assured of my salvation not *despite*
that experience but *because* of it.

In one sense, I've never recovered from those
desperate months. And I hope I never do.

Notes

1. J. I. Packer, *Knowing God* (Downers Grove, IL: Inter-Varsity Press, 1973), 112.
2. John Bunyan, *Grace Abounding to the Chief of Sinners*, ed. W. R. Owens (London: Penguin Books, 1987), 59.
3. Sinclair Ferguson, *Taking the Christian Life Seriously* (Grand Rapids, MI: Zondervan, 1981), 58.
4. John Webster, *Holiness* (Grand Rapids, MI: Eerdmans, 2003), 13.
5. Timothy Ward, *Words of Life: Scripture as the Living and Active Word of God* (Downers Grove, IL: IVP Academic, 2009), 23.

Scripture Index

IX 9Marks

Building Healthy Churches

9Marks exists to equip church leaders with a biblical vision and practical resources for displaying God's glory to the nations through healthy churches.

To that end, we want to see churches characterized by these nine marks of health:

1. Expositional Preaching
2. Gospel Doctrine
3. A Biblical Understanding of Conversion and Evangelism
4. Biblical Church Membership
5. Biblical Church Discipline
6. A Biblical Concern for Discipleship and Growth
7. Biblical Church Leadership
8. A Biblical Understanding of the Practice of Prayer
9. A Biblical Understanding and Practice of Missions

Find all our Crossway titles and other resources at 9Marks.org.

IX 9Marks Church Questions

Providing ordinary Christians with sound and
accessible biblical teaching by answering
common questions about church life.

For more information, visit crossway.org.